How To DRAW!®

DINOSAURS

Illustrated by
Georgene Griffin

Visit us at www.kidsbooks.com®

SUPPLIES

- NUMBER 2 PENCILS
- SOFT ERASER
- COLORED PENCILS
- MARKERS OR CRAYONS

HELPFUL HINTS

1. Take your time with steps 1 and 2.
Following the first steps carefully will make the final steps easier. The first two steps create a foundation of the figure—much like the frame of a house forms the foundation of the rest of the building. Next comes the fun part: creating the smooth, clean outline drawing of the dinosaur and adding all the finishing touches, details, shading, and color.

2. Always keep your pencil lines light and soft.
This will make your guidelines easier to erase when you no longer need them.

3. Don't be afraid to erase.
It usually takes a lot of drawing and erasing before you will be satisfied with the way your drawing looks.

4. Add details at the end.
Shading and finishing touches should be the last step *after* you have blended and refined all the shapes.

5. Remember: Practice makes perfect.
Don't be discouraged if you don't get the hang of it right away. Just keep drawing, erasing, and redrawing until you do.

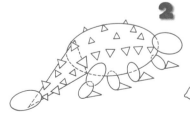

Palaeoscincus

(PAY-lee-oh-SKINK-us)

The name means "ancient skink," because the teeth resemble those of a modern skink (a type of lizard). Palaeoscincus was discovered when scientists found one of its teeth in Montana.

1 Begin this dinosaur with a large oval shape for the body and two overlapping circles for the head. Attach the tail, adding two egg-shaped ovals at the tip.

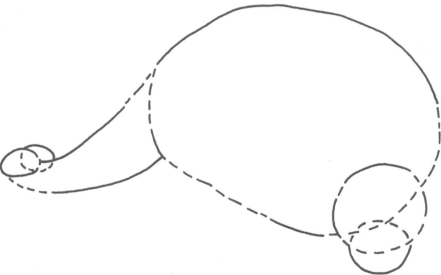

2 Add the legs and claws. Next, carefully add rows of triangle-shaped spikes all over the body and tail. Don't forget the four spikes protecting the head.

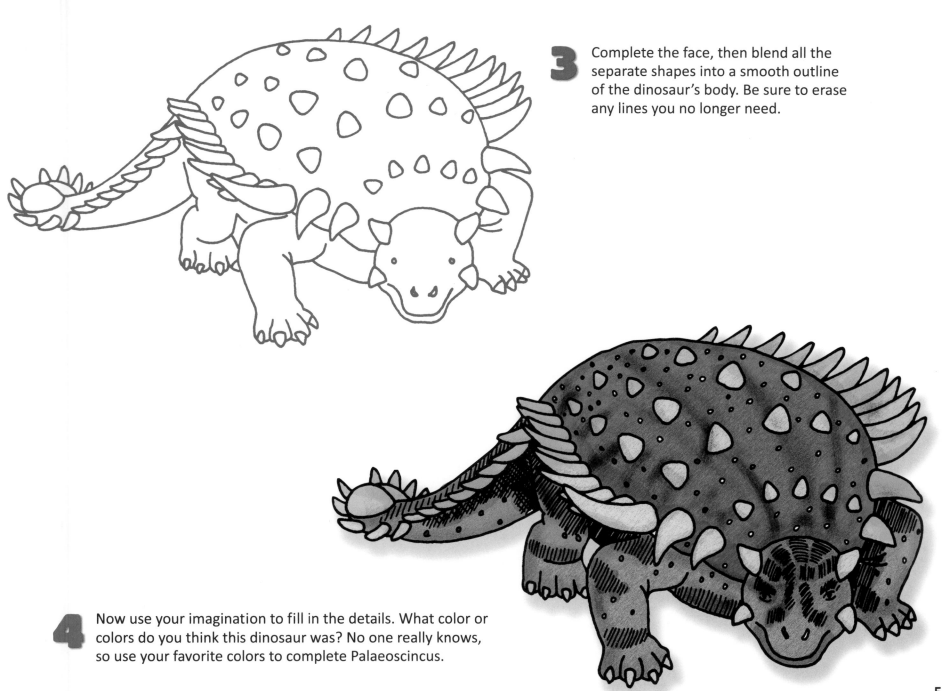

3 Complete the face, then blend all the separate shapes into a smooth outline of the dinosaur's body. Be sure to erase any lines you no longer need.

4 Now use your imagination to fill in the details. What color or colors do you think this dinosaur was? No one really knows, so use your favorite colors to complete Palaeoscincus.

Ornithomimus
(OR-nith-uh-MY-mus)

The name means "bird imitator," because this dinosaur resembled an ostrich. Ornithomimus was very speedy and ran quickly from danger.

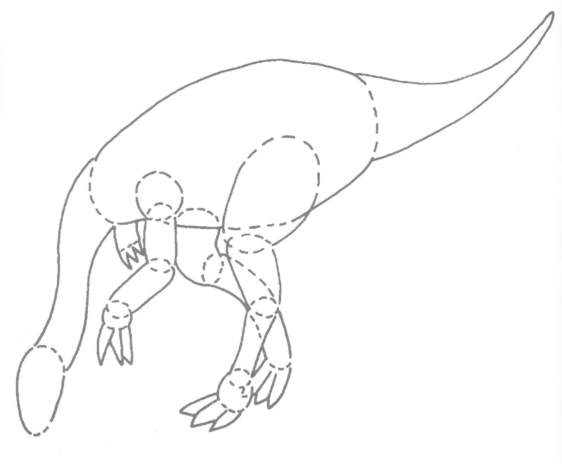

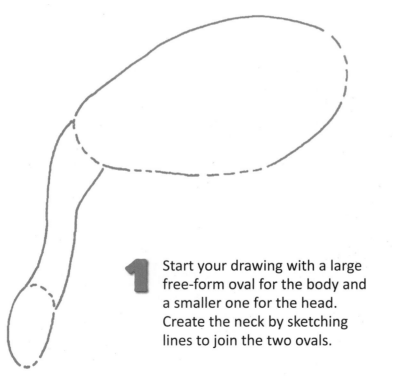

1 Start your drawing with a large free-form oval for the body and a smaller one for the head. Create the neck by sketching lines to join the two ovals.

2 Using simple basic shapes, draw the tail, arms, and legs, as shown.

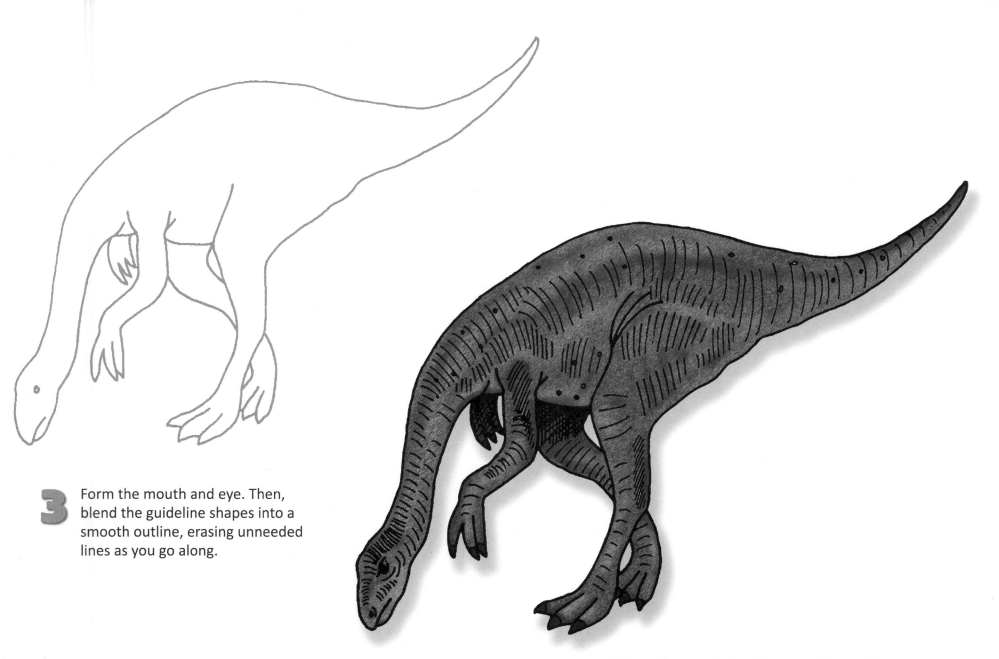

3 Form the mouth and eye. Then, blend the guideline shapes into a smooth outline, erasing unneeded lines as you go along.

 Add claws to the fingers and toes. Then, sketch lots of shading lines and skin texture for the finishing touches.

Diplodocus

(dih-PLOH-duh-kus)

The name, which means "double beam," refers to the Y-shaped vertebrae on the tail. A complete skeleton of Diplodocus measured 90 feet from head to tail. Many of this plant-eater's bones have been found in the Rocky Mountain states of North America.

2 Draw the rectangular-shaped legs and attach the huge, curved tail.

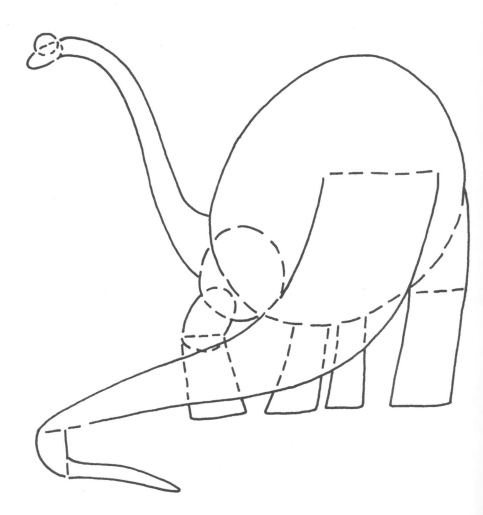

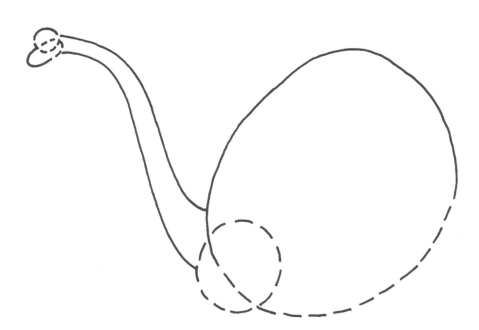

1 Start with a very large oval for the body. Add a small circle for the chest and a small oval with a circle on top for the head. Connect the head and body with two long, curving lines, forming the neck.

3 Add the eye and mouth. Then, blend all your shapes into one finished outline drawing. Erase any extra lines.

4 Add details, background, and color. You may want to create a scene by drawing several different dinosaurs in a prehistoric setting.

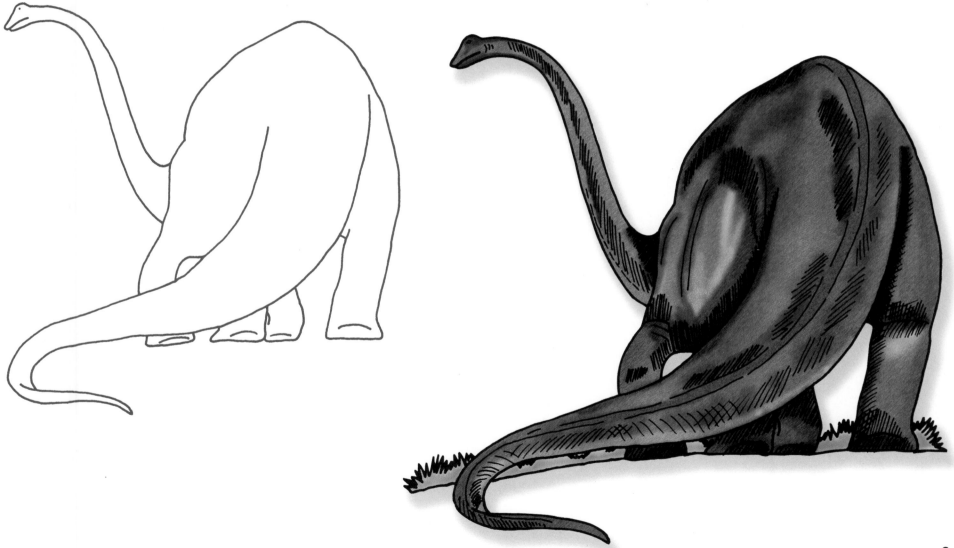

Velociraptor
(vuh-LAH-sih-RAP-tur)

The name means "swift robber," due to this dinosaur's quickness and its grasping hands. If Velociraptor was cold-blooded, its skin would have been similar to a lizard's. If it was warm-blooded, it may have been covered with feathers or fur.

1 Lightly sketch an egg-shaped oval for the body. Next, using oval guidelines, very carefully create the upper and lower jaws. Then connect them to the body, and add the tail.

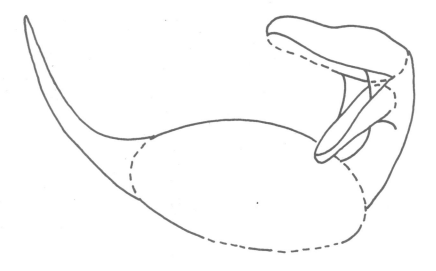

2 Using simple shapes, draw the arms, legs, and claws. Note the upturned claw on each foot.

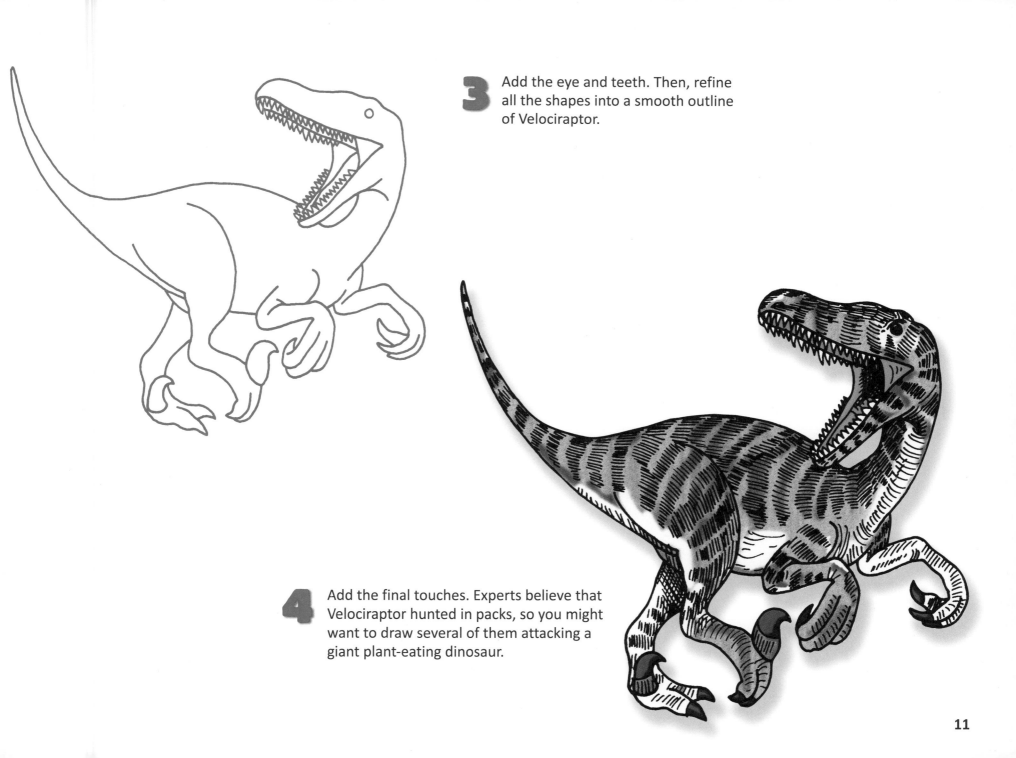

3 Add the eye and teeth. Then, refine all the shapes into a smooth outline of Velociraptor.

4 Add the final touches. Experts believe that Velociraptor hunted in packs, so you might want to draw several of them attacking a giant plant-eating dinosaur.

Coelophysis
(SEEL-uh-FYE-sis)

The name, which means "hollow form," refers to this dinosaur's hollow bones.

1 Start your drawing with basic shapes for the head, neck, body, arms, and legs.

2 Blend your shapes into a body form. Add a long, slender tail. Then, erase any lines you don't need.

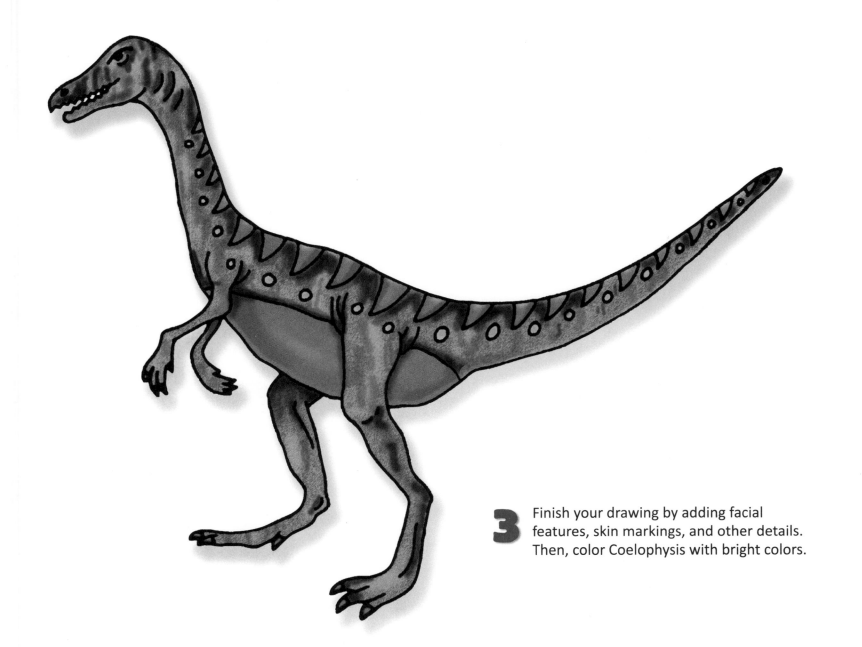

3 Finish your drawing by adding facial features, skin markings, and other details. Then, color Coelophysis with bright colors.

Hadrosaurus

(HAD-ruh-SORE-us)

The name means "bulky lizard," referring to the animal's big size. In 1868, a plaster skeleton of a Hadrosaurus was the first dinosaur model to ever be put on display.

2 Add a line for the mouth. Next, using ovals, rectangles, and triangles, add guideline shapes for the arms and legs.

1 Draw a large oval for the body and a smaller, pointy oval for the head. Connect the two ovals to form the neck. Then, attach a long triangle for the tail.

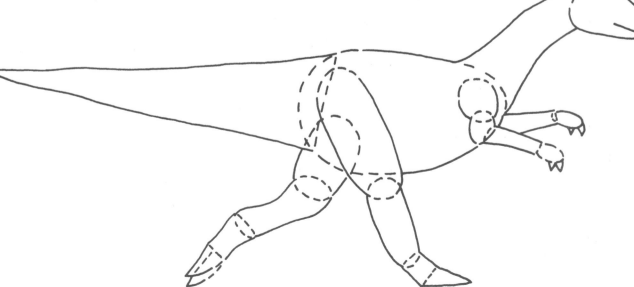

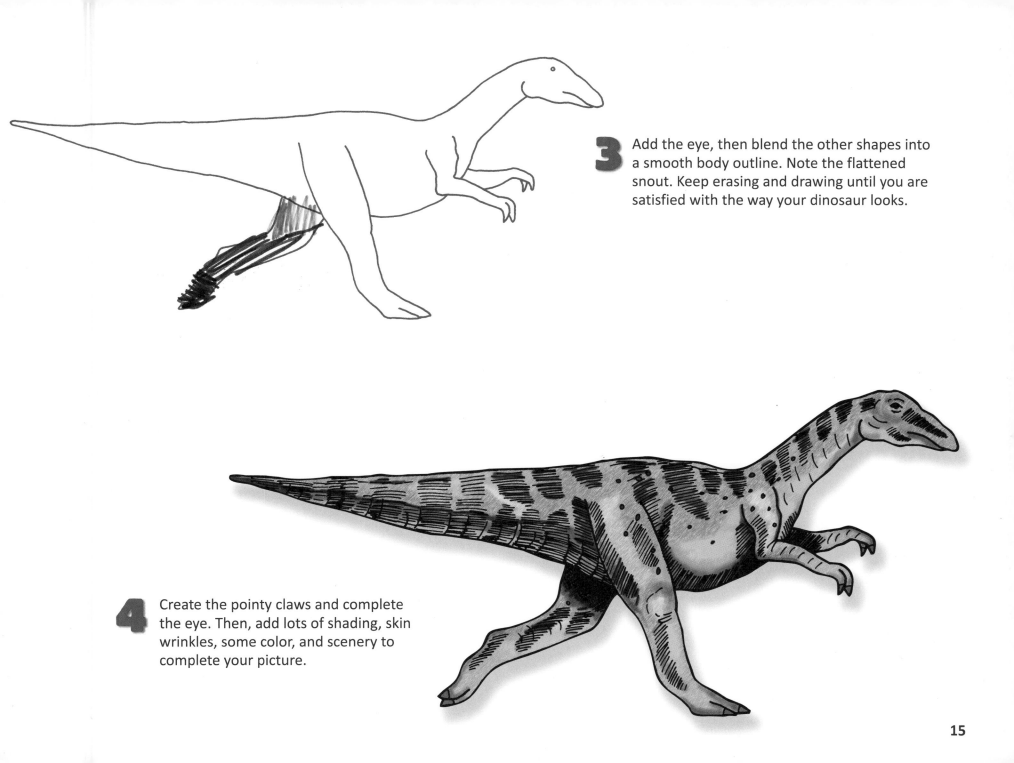

3 Add the eye, then blend the other shapes into a smooth body outline. Note the flattened snout. Keep erasing and drawing until you are satisfied with the way your dinosaur looks.

4 Create the pointy claws and complete the eye. Then, add lots of shading, skin wrinkles, some color, and scenery to complete your picture.

Iguanodon
(ih-GWAHN-uh-don)

The name means "iguana tooth," because the teeth resemble those of an iguana lizard. About 140 million years ago, a large number of Iguanodons drowned in a lake across northwest Europe. Many fossils have been found in this "Iguanodon graveyard."

1 Start with a large free-form oval for the body. Add a smaller oval for the head and a triangle shape for most of the neck. Connect the neck and body with a short line, as shown.

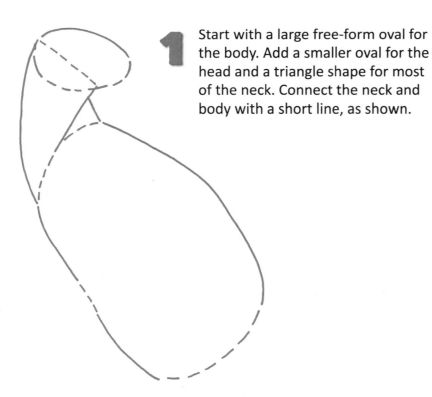

2 Add the basic shapes for the arms, legs, pointy claws, and tail. Note the spike pointing upward on top of each hand. Don't forget the mouth!

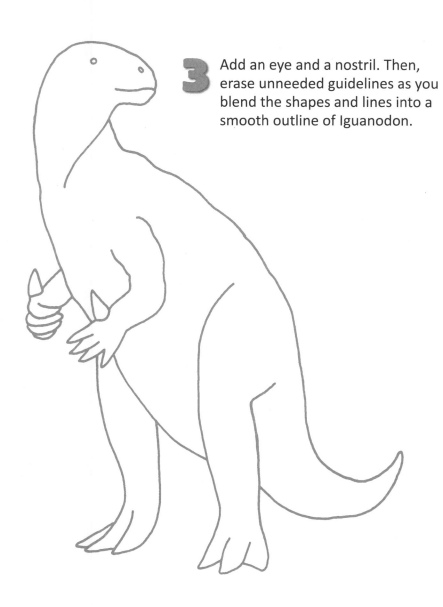

3 Add an eye and a nostril. Then, erase unneeded guidelines as you blend the shapes and lines into a smooth outline of Iguanodon.

4 Complete your drawing by adding rows of shading and skin details. Now this Iguanodon is ready to pound the prehistoric pavement!

Avimimus

(ah-vee-MEEM-us)

The name means "bird mimic," due to this dinosaur's birdlike appearance. Some experts believe that Avimimus was similar to the modern-day roadrunner, and that it might have had feathers.

2 Draw some simple shapes to create the arms, claws, legs, and feet. Shape the head and define the open mouth.

1 Lightly sketch a free-form shape for the body. Add the head, neck, and tail, as shown.

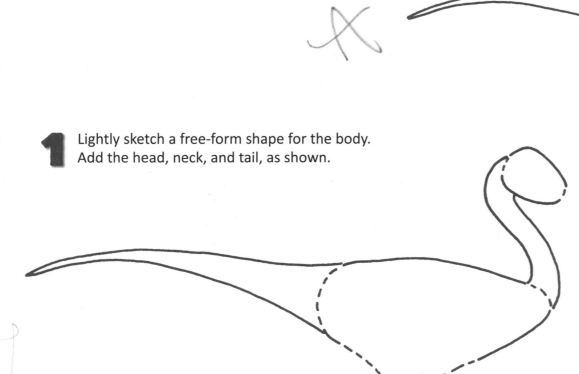

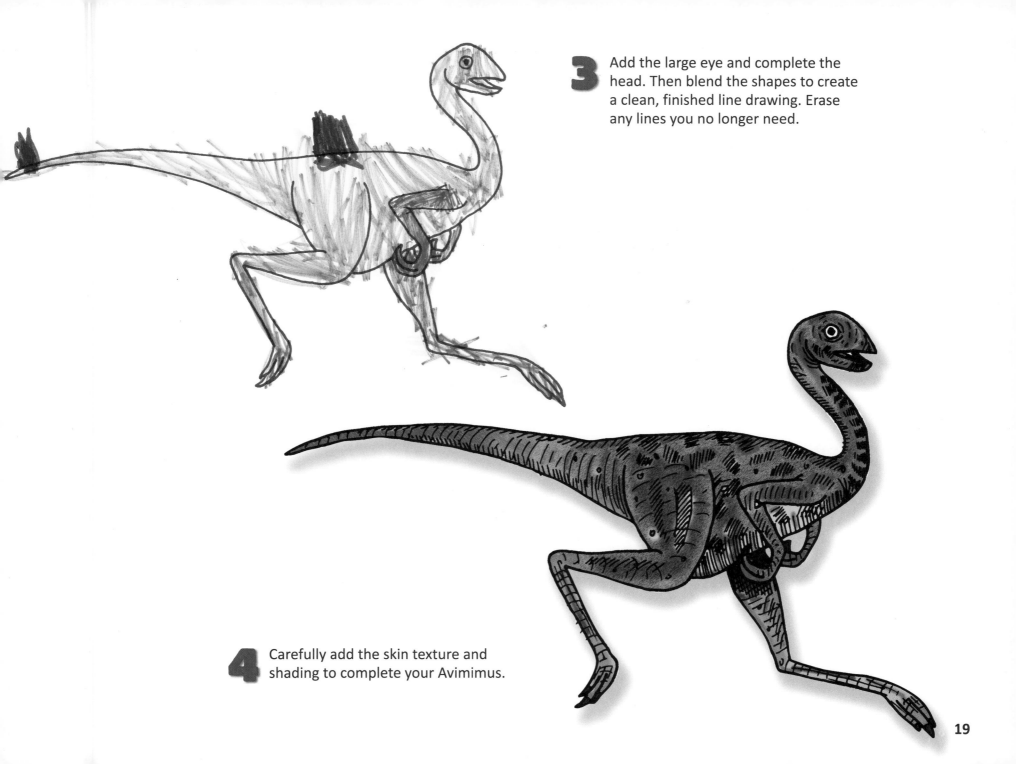

3 Add the large eye and complete the head. Then blend the shapes to create a clean, finished line drawing. Erase any lines you no longer need.

4 Carefully add the skin texture and shading to complete your Avimimus.

Tylosaurus

(TY-loh-SORE-us)

Tylosaurus—not a dinosaur—was one of the largest known seagoing lizards. Close in appearance to a modern crocodile, it was a hunter of fish and shellfish.

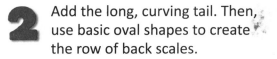

2 Add the long, curving tail. Then, use basic oval shapes to create the row of back scales.

1 Carefully draw the basic body shape. Add a small circle for the head and two triangles for the huge mouth. Next, add four ovals for the flippers, attaching them to the body with connector lines.

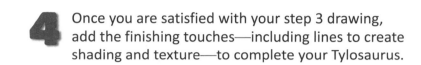

4 Once you are satisfied with your step 3 drawing, add the finishing touches—including lines to create shading and texture—to complete your Tylosaurus.

3 Add the teeth. Then, sketch and erase to blend all the shapes into a continuous body outline.

Lambeosaurus

(LAM-bee-uh-SORE-us)

The name means "Lambe's Lizard," in honor of Lawrence Lambe, who studied dinosaur fossils. Lambeosaurus was a crested duckbill dinosaur. The hollow crest on its head may have been used to make loud noises.

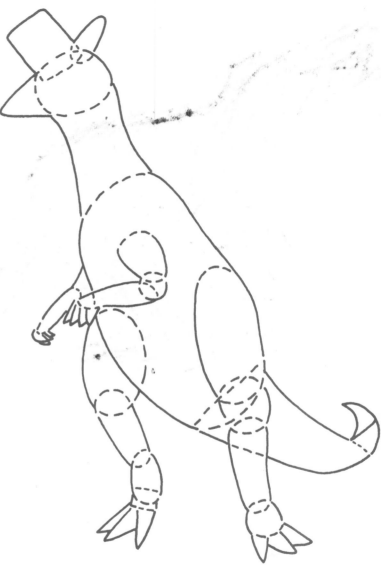

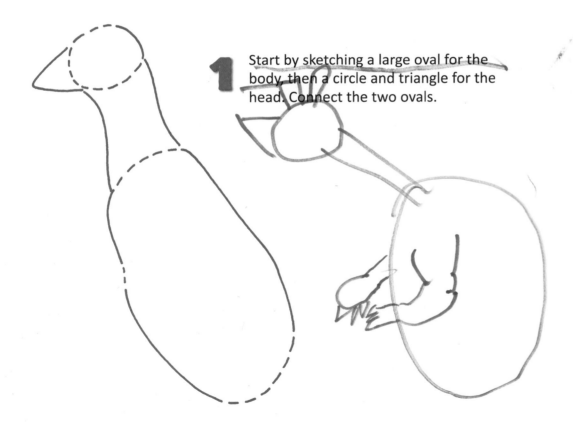

1 Start by sketching a large oval for the body, then a circle and triangle for the head. Connect the two ovals.

2 Carefully add the crest on top of the head with a rectangle and a small oval. Then, using basic guideline shapes, lightly sketch the arms, hands, legs, feet, and tail.

3 Add the eye, nostril, and mouth. Blend the guideline shapes into a smooth outline of the dinosaur's body, erasing any lines you no longer need.

4 Add shading, texture, and other finishing touches to complete your Lambeosaurus.

Allosaurus
(AL-uh-SORE-us)

The name means "different lizard," because the bones of the spine were different from other dinosaurs.' Allosaurus was a big, 40-foot-long, meat-eating dinosaur. It was quite active for its size.

1 Start your drawing with a large, bean-shaped oval for the body. Lightly sketch a smaller oval for the head, then connect them to form the neck. Then, add a small oval guideline where the eye will go.

2 Draw the open mouth. Then, using basic shapes, carefully attach the arms, legs, and tail.

3 Add the teeth and eye. Then, blend the lines and shapes into a smooth, clean outline. As you work, erase any guidelines you no longer need.

4 Finish Allosaurus by adding lots of detail. Shading, lines for wrinkles, and tiny shapes for the bumpy skin texture will give your drawing a realistic look. Don't forget some background scenery.

Chasmosaurus
(KAZ-moh-SORE-us)

The name means "opening lizard," describing the openings in this dinosaur's head frill. The large holes lightened the bony frill's weight. A plant-eater, Chasmosaurus was one of the most widespread dinosaurs.

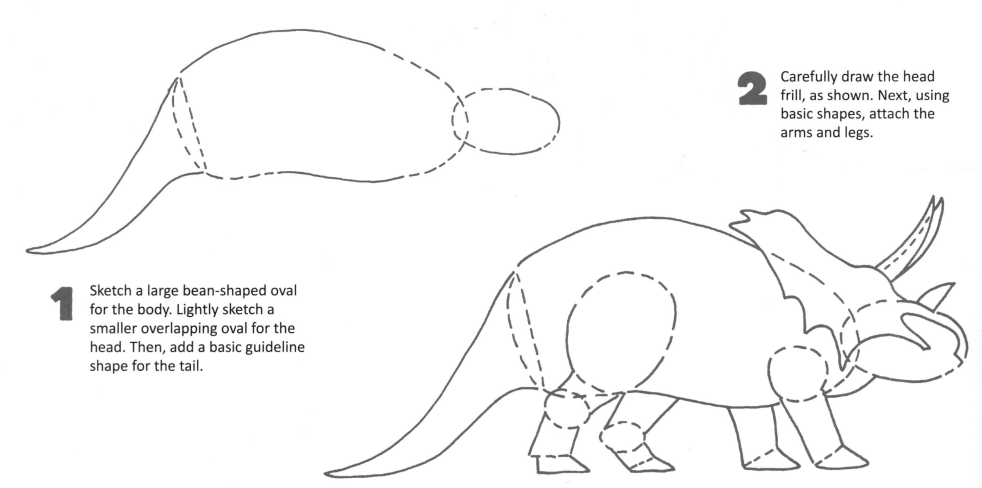

2 Carefully draw the head frill, as shown. Next, using basic shapes, attach the arms and legs.

1 Sketch a large bean-shaped oval for the body. Lightly sketch a smaller overlapping oval for the head. Then, add a basic guideline shape for the tail.

3 Add an eye, then create the open mouth and nostril. Next, add two overlapping horns on the frill, and a smaller horn on the front of the head. Blend the shapes into a smooth, clean outline. Erase any unneeded guidelines.

4 Finish Chasmosaurus by adding lots of shading and detail. Now this dinosaur is ready to go hunting for some food!

Archaeopteryx
(AR-kee-OP-ter-iks)

The name means "ancient wing" because many experts believe that this animal was one of the first birds. Archaeopteryx fossils found in limestone in Germany show impressions of long feathers on the wings and tail.

1 Draw an oval for the body, then a small circle for the head. Connect them to form the neck. Then, add two overlapping triangles for the beak.

 **2** Add three large guideline shapes for the wings and tail feathers. Then, add claws, which stick out at the front of each wing.

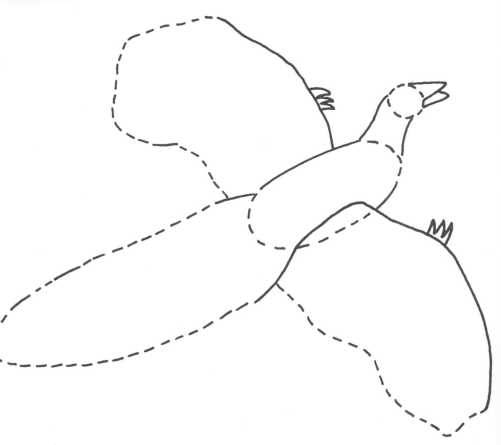

3 Carefully form curved feathers around the edges of the wings and tail. Next, draw dotted lines on each wing as shown. Add the eye and nostril. Then, blend the shapes into one smooth body outline, erasing any lines you no longer need.

4 Add two more rows of feathers to each wing. This part is fun to do! Make the outer wing and tail feathers longer. Then, add shading and details to complete your drawing.

Ouranosaurus

(oo-RAN-oh-SORE-us)

The name means "valiant lizard," after a West African word for "fearless." A relative of Iguanodon, Ouranosaurus had a sail on its back, probably to keep it from overheating.

1 Start with a large, free-form oval for the body. Add the head and pointed "beak," then connect them to the body. Next, use simple shapes to draw the arms and legs.

2 Attach a long, curvy tail. Then, create the sail by sketching a line from behind the head to halfway down the tail. Add oval shapes to the sail, as shown.

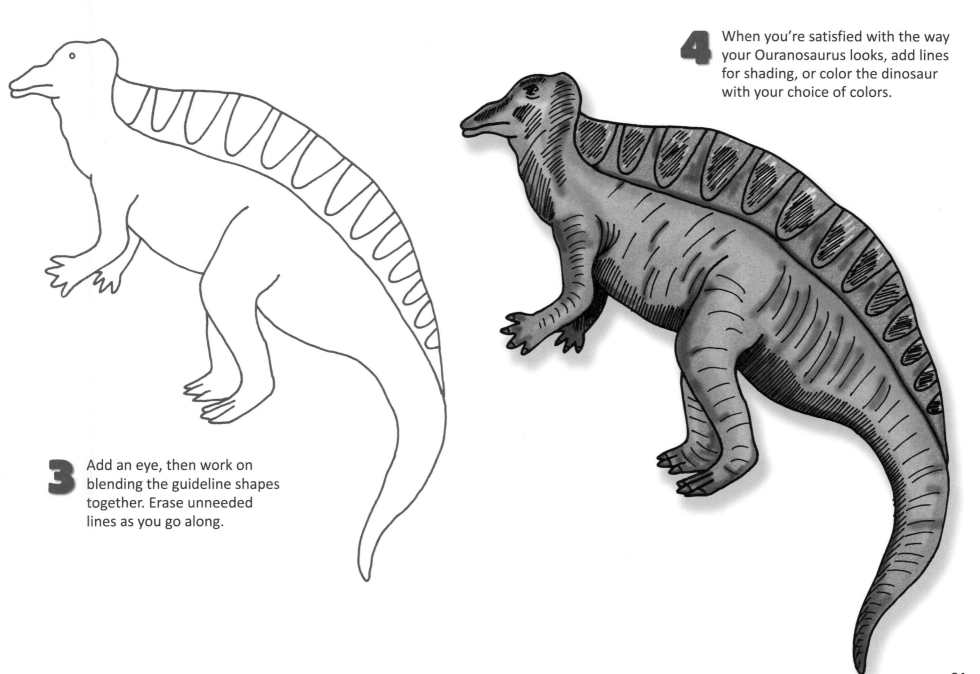

4 When you're satisfied with the way your Ouranosaurus looks, add lines for shading, or color the dinosaur with your choice of colors.

3 Add an eye, then work on blending the guideline shapes together. Erase unneeded lines as you go along.

Brachiosaurus
(BRAK-ee-uh-SORE-us)

The name means "arm lizard," referring to the long front legs. The tiny head of Brachiosaurus had huge nostrils on top. They may have helped to keep the dinosaur cool.

1 Lightly sketch the basic guideline shapes—ovals, rectangles, and triangles—for the body, legs, and feet.

2 High above the body, draw the head, using a small oval and a circle. Connect the head to the body with two long curved lines. Then, use more simple, basic shapes to add the tail.

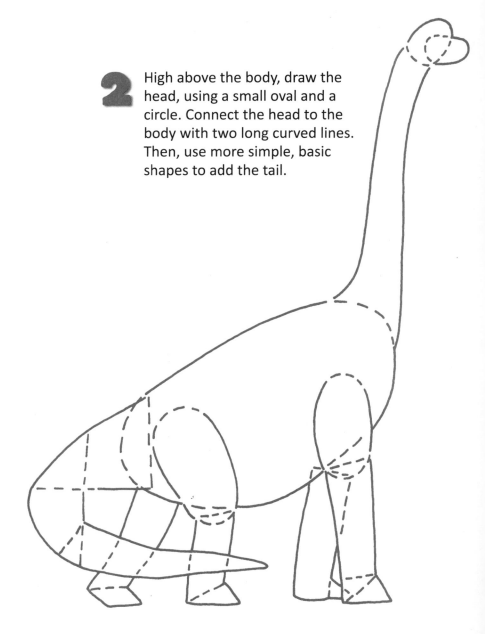

3 Add the mouth and eye. Blend the shapes into a continuous smooth outline, erasing unnecessary guidelines as you go along.

4 Lots of interesting shading will make your Brachiosaurus come alive. What color do you think this dinosaur was?

Megalosaurus
(MEG-ah-loh-SORE-us)

The name, which means "big lizard," refers to this animal's size. Megalosaurus was the first dinosaur to be described and named, early in the 19th century.

2 Add the basic shapes for the legs and tail. Then, sketch and erase to create the open mouth, as shown.

1 Begin by drawing the basic shapes for the body and head. Sketch lines to connect the head and body, forming the neck. Add more basic shapes for the arms and hands.

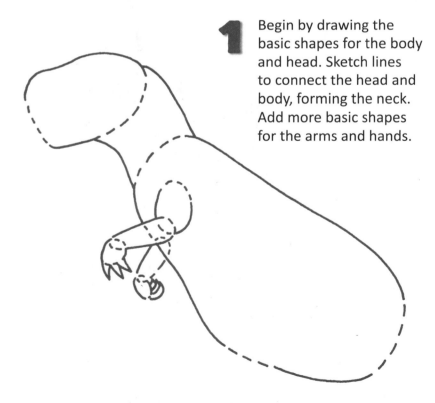

4 Add details and shading to complete this fierce-looking, meat-eating dinosaur.

3 Add the eye and sharp teeth. Next, blend all the shapes together, erasing any lines you no longer need. Make sure you are satisfied with the way the outline drawing looks before going to step 4.

Dilophosaurus
(dye-LOH-fuh-SORE-us)

The name means "two-crested lizard" because of the two crests on this dinosaur's head. Unlike other big meat-eaters, Dilophosaurus had bone joints that would have allowed it to wrinkle its nose.

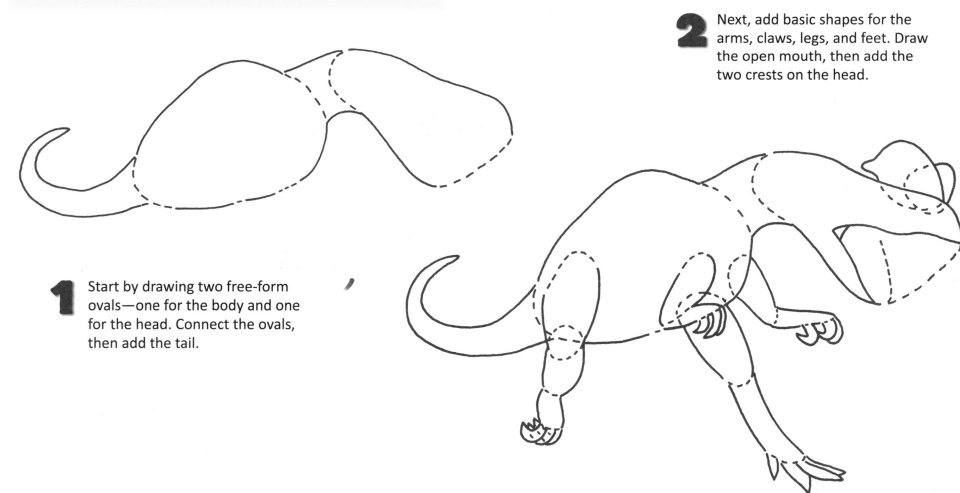

2 Next, add basic shapes for the arms, claws, legs, and feet. Draw the open mouth, then add the two crests on the head.

1 Start by drawing two free-form ovals—one for the body and one for the head. Connect the ovals, then add the tail.

3 Add an eye and a nostril. Blend the lines and shapes into a smooth outline of Dilophosaurus. Then, add lots of pointy teeth.

4 Now add all the final touches. Spots, shading, and skin wrinkles will make this dinosaur look ferociously real.

Hylaeosaurus

(HY-lee-oh-SORE-us)

The name means "wood lizard," because of the place in England where it was found. Armored Hylaeosaurus lived near a body of water that formed as the continents drifted apart during the early Cretaceous period.

1 Draw a large, free-form oval as the basic guideline shape for the body. Draw a smaller overlapping oval for the head. Add more simple shapes for the legs, feet, and tail.

2 Add an oval for the mouth and a circle for the snout. Then, sketching carefully, add the rows of triangular spikes on the dinosaur's back and tail.

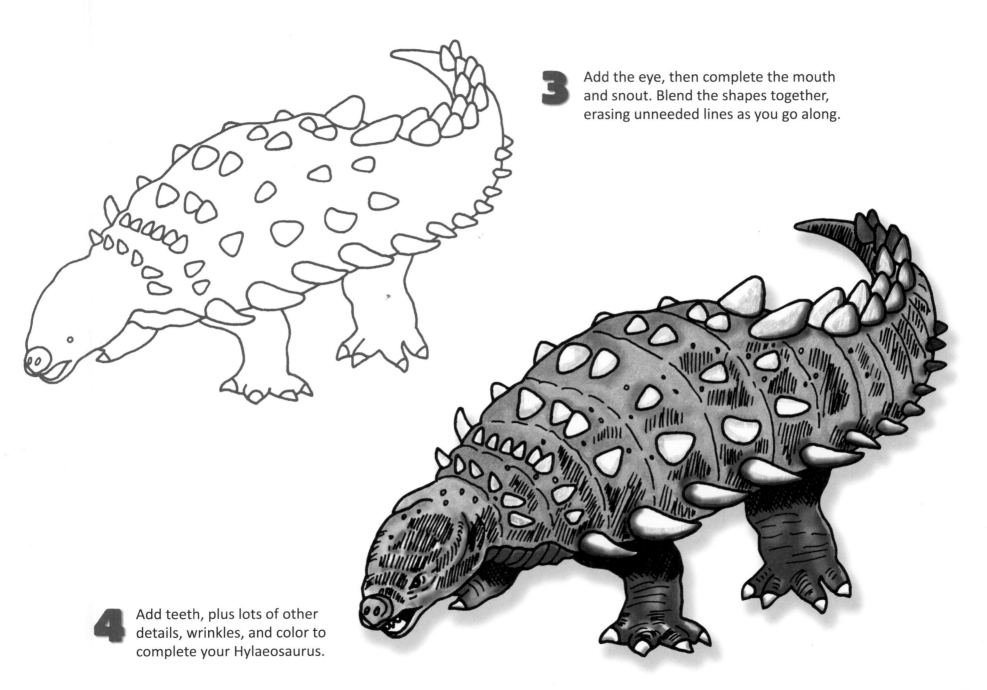

3 Add the eye, then complete the mouth and snout. Blend the shapes together, erasing unneeded lines as you go along.

4 Add teeth, plus lots of other details, wrinkles, and color to complete your Hylaeosaurus.

Deinonychus
(dye-NON-ih-kus)

The name means "terrible claw" because of the giant, curved claw on top of each foot. Wolf-sized Deinonychus, a meat-eater, may have hunted in packs.

2 Create the mouth. Then, using simple guideline shapes, sketch the arms, legs, and claws. Note the large, curved claw on top of each foot.

1 Draw a large oval for the body, then a smaller oval for the head. Connect the two ovals to form the neck. Attach a long triangle for the tail.

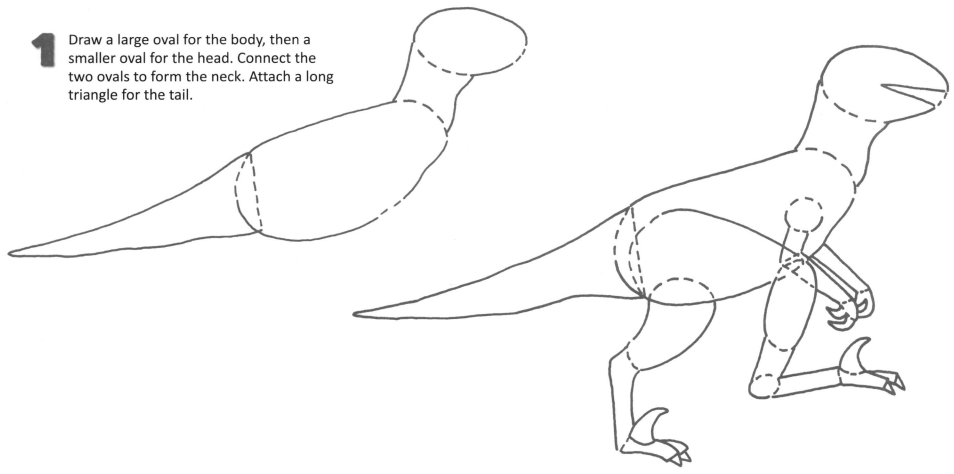

3 Add the eye, nostril, and sharp teeth. Starting with the head, blend the shapes into an outline drawing of this fierce, meat-eating dinosaur. Keep drawing, erasing, and redrawing until you are satisfied.

4 Now add the finishing touches. Careful use of shading, skin texture, and color will make Deinonychus come alive!

Albertosaurus
(al-BUR-tuh-SORE-us)

The name means "Alberta lizard," after the area in Canada where it was found. A relative of Tyrannosaurus, Albertosaurus is also known as Gorgosaurus.

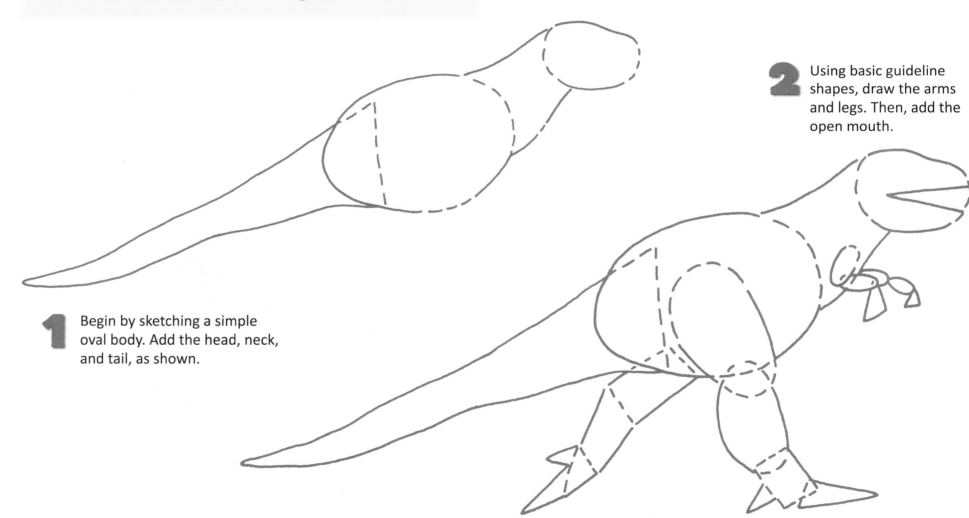

1 Begin by sketching a simple oval body. Add the head, neck, and tail, as shown.

2 Using basic guideline shapes, draw the arms and legs. Then, add the open mouth.

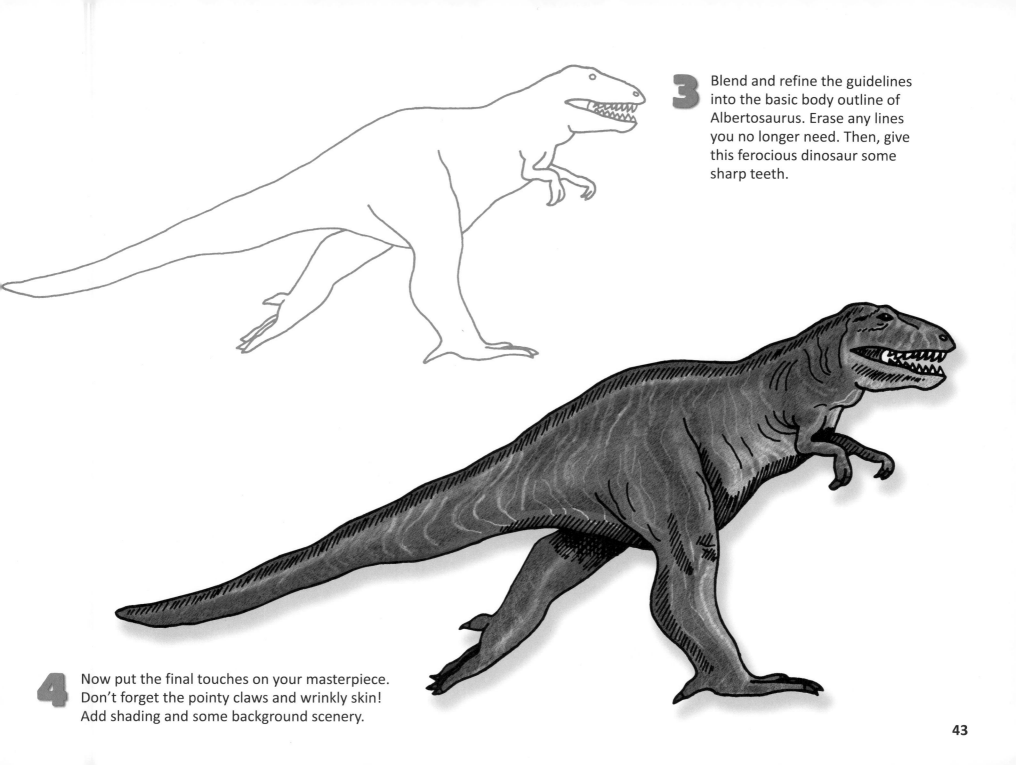

3 Blend and refine the guidelines into the basic body outline of Albertosaurus. Erase any lines you no longer need. Then, give this ferocious dinosaur some sharp teeth.

4 Now put the final touches on your masterpiece. Don't forget the pointy claws and wrinkly skin! Add shading and some background scenery.

APATOSAURUS
(uh-PAT-uh-SORE-us)

The name means "deceptive lizard." At one time, this dinosaur was known as Brontosaurus.

1 Start with a large, oval body and legs. Add a long neck with a small, oval head. Then, add a long tail.

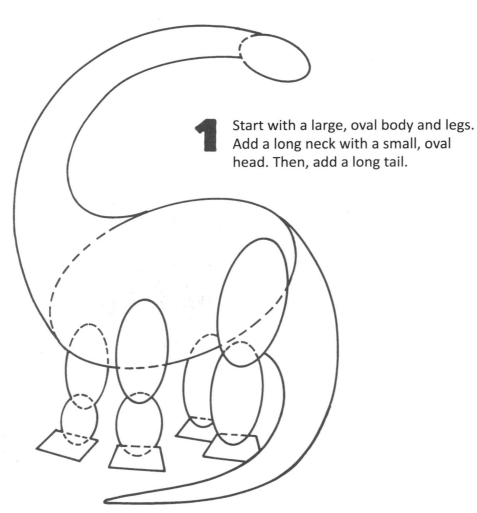

2 Blend all your shapes into one body shape. Erase any unnecessary lines.

3 Add lots of detail, shading, and texture. Put wrinkles on the skin surface too! Draw some background scenery to complete your drawing.

CORYTHOSAURUS

(koh-RITH-oh-SORE-us)

The name, which means "helmet lizard," refers to the shape of the bony crest on this dinosaur's head.

2 Next, add guidelines for the tail, legs, arms, and mouth. Corythosaurus had a mouth that looked like a duck's beak, and large, powerful legs to support its body.

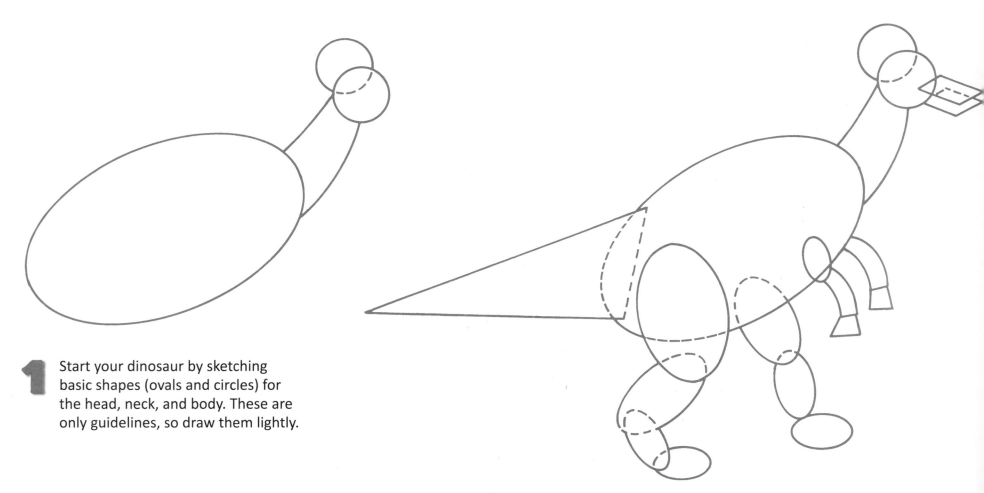

1 Start your dinosaur by sketching basic shapes (ovals and circles) for the head, neck, and body. These are only guidelines, so draw them lightly.

3 Blend the basic shapes into a clean outline, erasing guidelines that you no longer need.

4 For the final step, add all the details. Draw in skin patterns, an eye, some claws, and skin folds. Then, use your imagination to add some color.

TYRANNOSAURUS
(ty-RAN-uh-SORE-us)

The name, which means "tyrant lizard," refers to its huge size and sharp teeth—signs that it was a fierce and mighty predator. It was one of the largest meat-eating dinosaurs.

2 Using basic shapes as your guide, add small forearms and large legs, as shown.

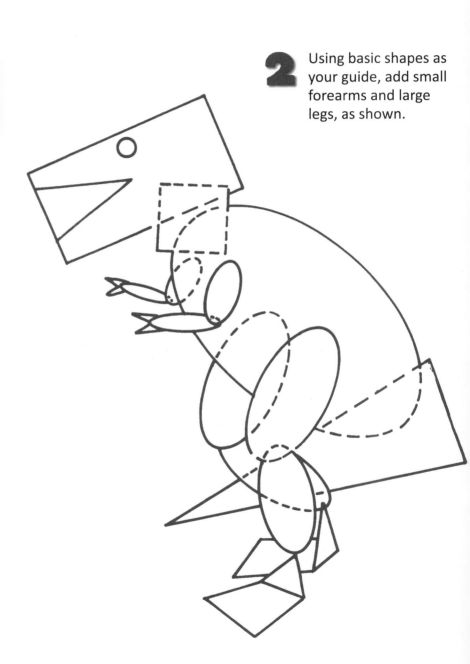

1 Use rectangles, ovals, squares, and triangles for the basic body, head, and tail. These are only guidelines, so draw them lightly.

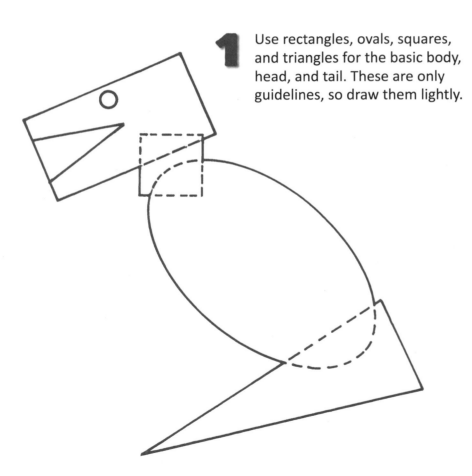

4 Put all the finishing touches on your drawing. Give Tyrannosaurus a ferocious look, big teeth, a mean look in its eye, and lots of skin effects.

3 Use your guidelines to form a clean outline of the basic body shape. As you work, erase any lines you don't need.

STEGOSAURUS
(STEG-uh-SORE-us)

The name, which means "plated lizard," refers to the rows of plates on this dinosaur's back.

1 Start drawing your Stegosaurus by lightly sketching these basic shapes: first, a large oval, then two smaller ovals and a triangle.

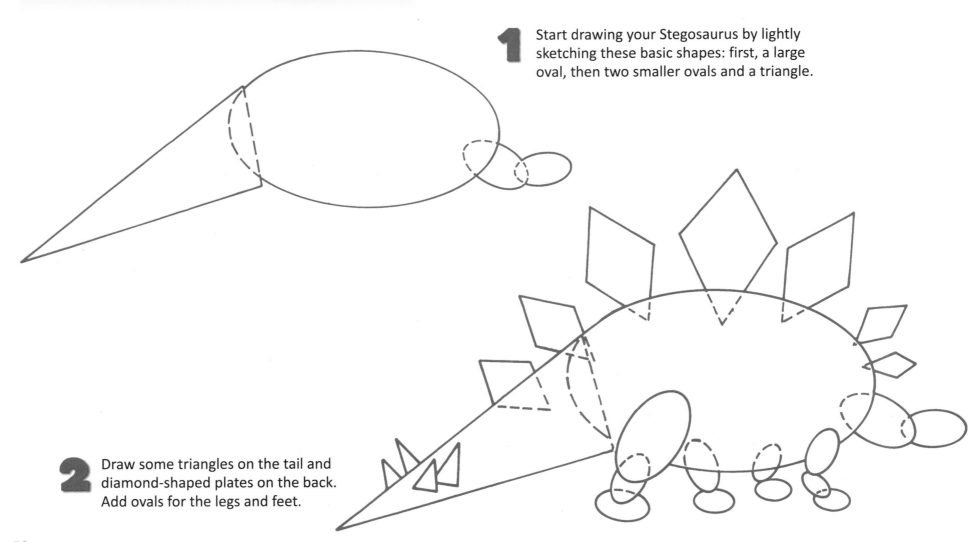

2 Draw some triangles on the tail and diamond-shaped plates on the back. Add ovals for the legs and feet.

3 Take all your guidelines and blend them into this dinosaur's basic shape. Erase any unnecessary lines so that you have a clean line drawing of your Stegosaurus.

4 Put the finishing touches on your drawing. Add texture to the back plates and some spots to Stegosaurus's back.

PARASAUROLOPHUS
(pah-ruh-saw-RAHL-uh-fus)

The name means "similar-crested lizard." No one knows the purpose of the bony crest on this dinosaur's head. Some experts think that it helped the animal's sense of smell. Others think that it was used to make loud noises.

2 Add a long, triangular tail, then ovals for the two forearms. Sketch and erase until you are satisfied with all of these basic guideline shapes.

1 Start your drawing with a large oval for the body. Add legs and feet, then an oval neck and triangular head. Draw curving guidelines for a long, bony crest on the head.

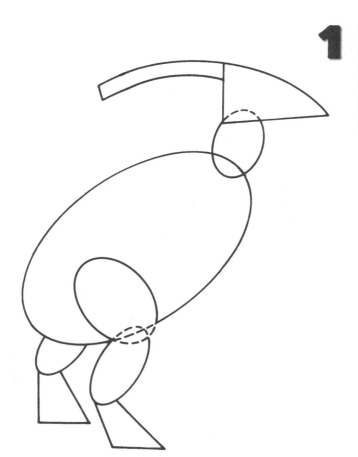

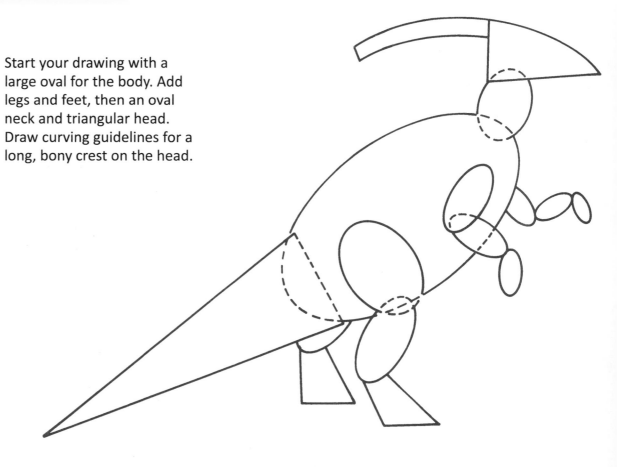

3 Now blend all your guideline shapes into a clean outline of the body frame.

4 Add claws, an eye, a nostril, and lots of skin folds, shading, and texture.

Ankylosaurus

(ANG-kye-luh-SORE-us)

The name, which means "stiffened lizard," refers to this animal's hard, armor-plated body surface.

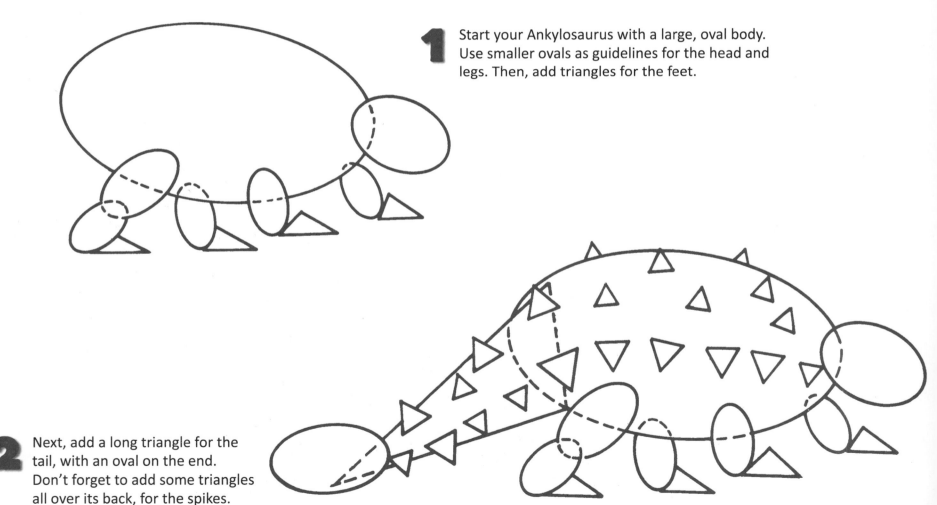

1 Start your Ankylosaurus with a large, oval body. Use smaller ovals as guidelines for the head and legs. Then, add triangles for the feet.

2 Next, add a long triangle for the tail, with an oval on the end. Don't forget to add some triangles all over its back, for the spikes.

3 Add more bumps to the back as you refine the outline shape and erase guidelines.

4 Finish your drawing by adding claws, an eye, skin texture, and other details.

PTERANODON

(terr-AN-oh-dahn)

The name means "winged and toothless," because this animal could fly and had no teeth. Pteranodon was not a dinosaur—it was a Late Cretaceous flying reptile with a 25-foot wingspan.

2 Next, draw guideline shapes for the arms, claws, and legs.

1 Start your drawing with simple shapes, as shown. Be sure to draw the wings much longer than the body.

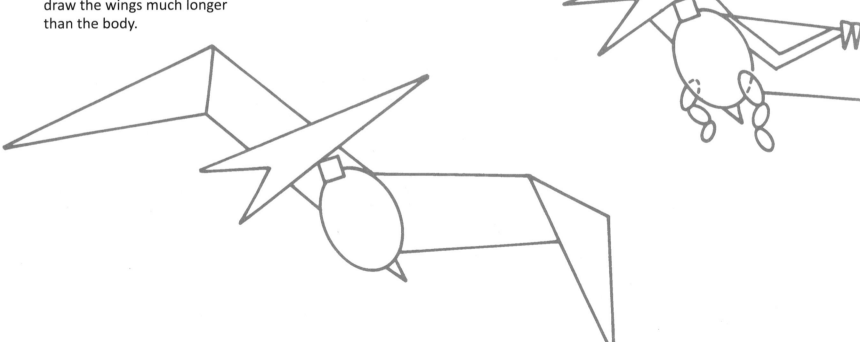

3 Sketch and erase to refine your drawing. Then, add the finishing details.

PACHYCEPHALOSAURUS
(pak-ee-SEFF-uh-loh-SORE-us)

The name, which means "reptile with a thick head," refers to the 10-inch-thick bone on top of this animal's head. Experts think that this dinosaur used its thick skull in head-butting contests.

1 Start by sketching the oval body, then add guideline shapes for the head, neck, and tail.

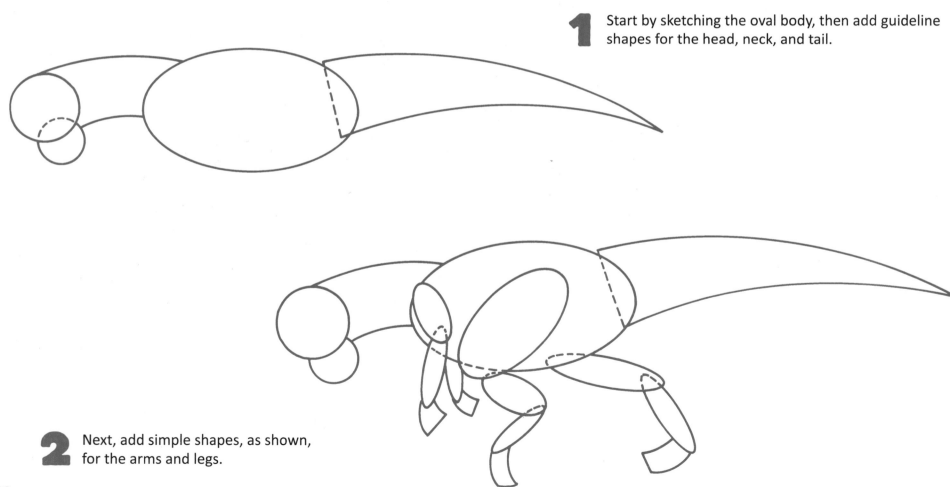

2 Next, add simple shapes, as shown, for the arms and legs.

3 Sketch and erase to blend the separate guideline shapes into a clean outline of the body frame. Keep the head, neck, back, and tail in a straight line—this dinosaur is posed in head-butting position. As you work, erase unneeded guidelines.

4 Now add the finishing touches: some spots on the skin; bony, bumpy texture on the head and nose; and lots of skin wrinkles. Why not add some scenery—and a second Pachycephalosaurus facing this one, ready for battle?

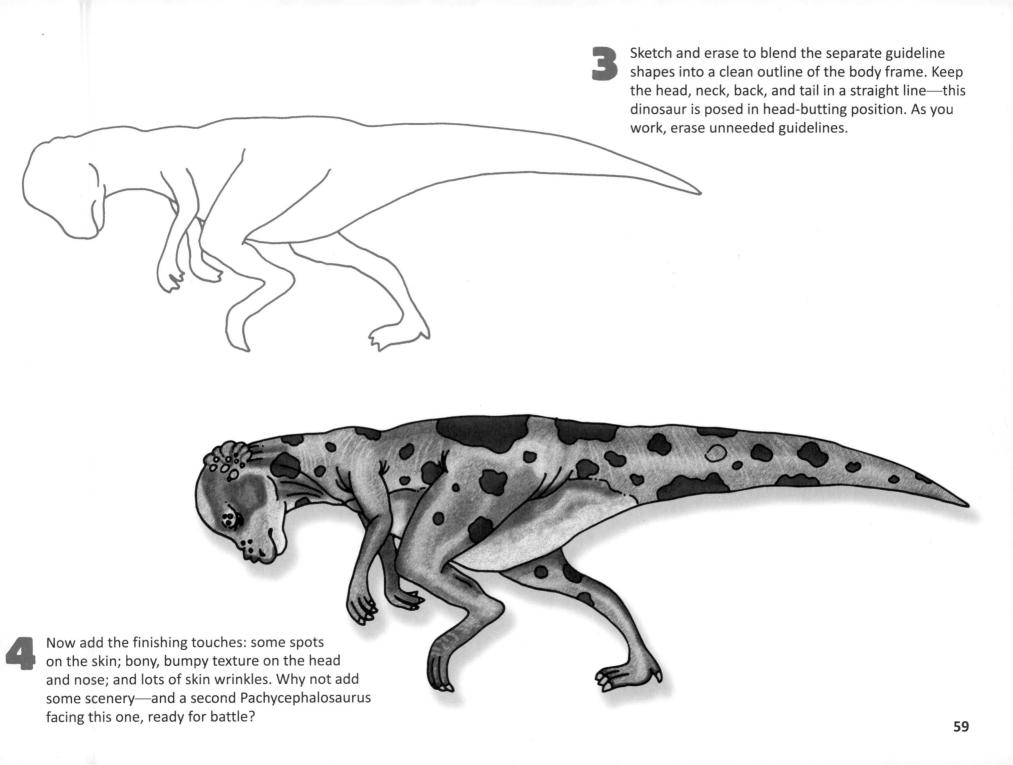

TRICERATOPS

(try-SER-uh-tops)

The name means "three-horned face." This animal was one of the last dinosaurs to become extinct.

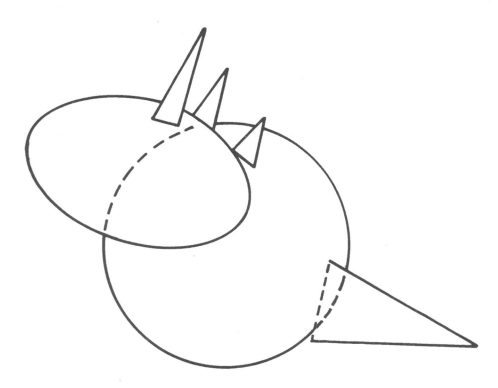

1 Start drawing by sketching a large circle for the body. Then, add an oval and triangles, as shown.

2 Add four legs using ovals and triangles. See how the legs bend where these shapes meet? Then, add some small triangles around the back of the head.

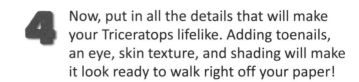

4 Now, put in all the details that will make your Triceratops lifelike. Adding toenails, an eye, skin texture, and shading will make it look ready to walk right off your paper!

3 Using your basic shapes as a guide, create a more realistic shape. Erase any extra lines that you don't need.

SPINOSAURUS

(SPY-nuh-SORE-us)

The name, which means "spiny lizard," refers to the long, 6-foot spines on this dinosaur's back.

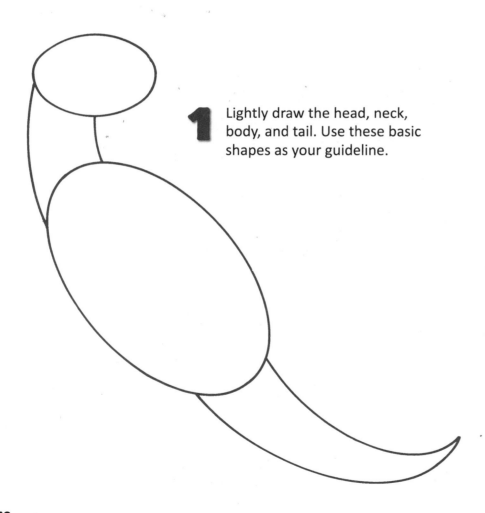

1 Lightly draw the head, neck, body, and tail. Use these basic shapes as your guideline.

2 Add arms, legs, and a guideline for the row of spines on the Spinosaurus's back. Keep all guidelines light, so they will be easy to erase later.

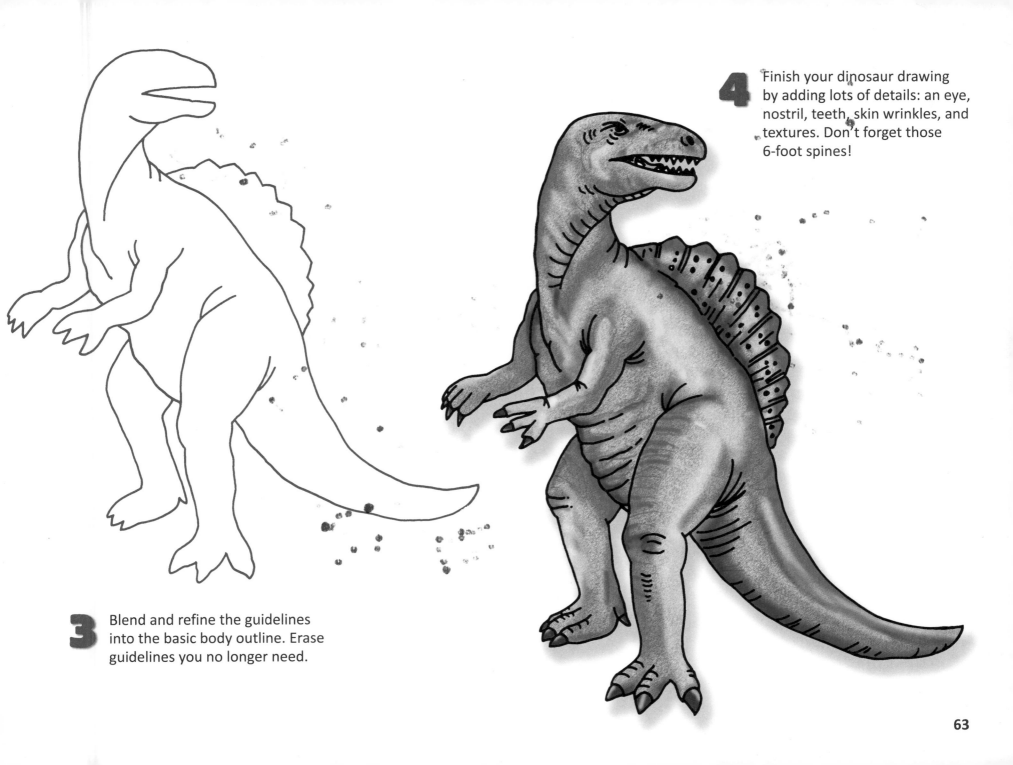

4 Finish your dinosaur drawing by adding lots of details: an eye, nostril, teeth, skin wrinkles, and textures. Don't forget those 6-foot spines!

3 Blend and refine the guidelines into the basic body outline. Erase guidelines you no longer need.